ROBERT BURNS

'A Red, Red Rose'
and other poems

ROBERT BURNS
'A Red, Red Rose'
and other poems

Selected and introduced by
DOMINIQUE ENRIGHT

Michael O'Mara Books Limited

First published in Great Britain in 2002 by
Michael O'Mara Books Limited
9 Lion Yard, Tremadoc Road
London SW4 7NQ

A CIP catalogue record for this book is available from the British Library

The text of Burns's poems as printed here follows accepted
available editions

ISBN 1-85479-767-0

1 3 5 7 9 10 8 6 4 2

Designed and typeset by Martin Bristow
Printed and bound in Finland by WS Bookwell, Juva

CONTENTS

INTRODUCTION

IN A TRAGICALLY SHORT LIFE, Robert Burns (1759–96) forged for himself a reputation as a poet and songwriter that has never been eclipsed. Today he is widely accepted as the greatest of all Scottish poets, and his verse remains among the most popular in the world. He has the distinction, even above Shakespeare, of being the world's most translated poet.

Born the son of a smallholder, Burns was entirely self-educated – no mean task for a farm labourer. A wide knowledge of, and an assured ear for, old Scots verse and songs led to publication of his early poems in 1786. The collection's huge popularity made the twenty-seven-year-old a social as well as a literary sensation, and assured the publication of later volumes of poetry, as well as collections of old Scottish songs, with their music. His skill in employing conversational rhythms in poetry has always made his verse enormously accessible, despite his widespread use of the Scots vernacular, and he is best known for his dialect lyrical verse on nature, love, patriotism, and rural life, as well as for such well-loved songs as 'Auld Lang Syne' and 'Robert Bruce's March To Bannockburn' – better known as 'Scots, Wha Hae'. This little collection celebrates the work of the poor farmer-turned-exciseman who became, literally, the voice of an entire nation, a poet who was as skilful with bawdy ballads as he was with great lyrics on philosophical subjects.

Song: Mary Morison
(1780)

O Mary, at thy window be,
It is the wish'd, the trysted hour;
Those smiles and glances let me see,
That make the miser's treasure poor:
How blythely wad I bide the stoure,
A weary slave frae sun to sun,
Could I the rich reward secure,
The lovely Mary Morison.

Yestreen, when to the trembling string
The dance gaed thro' the lighted ha',
To thee my fancy took its wing,
I sat, but neither heard nor saw:
Tho' this was fair, and that was braw,
And yon the toast of a' the town,
I sigh'd, and said amang them a',
'Ye are na Mary Morison.'

O, Mary, canst thou wreck his peace,
Wha for thy sake wad gladly die!
Or canst thou break that heart of his,
Whase only faut is loving thee.

If love for love thou wilt na gie,
At least be pity to me shown;
A thought ungentle canna be
The thought o' Mary Morison.

Winter: A Dirge
(1781)

The wintry west extends his blast,
And hail and rain does blaw;
Or the stormy north sends driving forth
The blinding sleet and snaw:
While, tumbling brown, the burn comes down,
And roars frae bank to brae;
And bird and beast in covert rest,
And pass the heartless day.

'The sweeping blast, the sky o'ercast,'
The joyless winter day
Let others fear, to me more dear
Than all the pride of May:
The tempest's howl, it soothes my soul,
My griefs it seems to join;
The leafless trees my fancy please,
Their fate resembles mine!

Thou Power Supreme, whose mighty scheme
These woes of mine fulfil,
Here firm I rest; they must be best,
Because they are Thy will!
Then all I want – O do Thou grant
This one request of mine! –
Since to enjoy Thou dost deny,
Assist me to resign.

Prayer, in the Prospect of Death
(1781)

O Thou unknown, Almighty Cause
Of all my hope and fear!
In whose dread presence, ere an hour,
Perhaps I must appear!

If I have wander'd in those paths
Of life I ought to shun,
As something, loudly, in my breast,
Remonstrates I have done;

Thou know'st that Thou hast formed me
With passions wild and strong;
And list'ning to their witching voice
Has often led me wrong.

Where human weakness has come short,
Or frailty stept aside,
Do Thou, All-Good – for such Thou art –
In shades of darkness hide.

Where with intention I have err'd,
No other plea I have,
But, Thou art good; and Goodness still
Delighteth to forgive.

Fickle Fortune: a Fragment
(1782)

Though fickle Fortune has deceived me,
She promis'd fair and perform'd but ill;
Of mistress, friends, and wealth bereav'd me,
Yet I bear a heart shall support me still.

I'll act with prudence as far's I'm able,
But if success I must never find,
Then come misfortune, I bid thee welcome,
I'll meet thee with an undaunted mind.

Impromptu – I'll Go and be a Sodger
(1782)

O why the deuce should I repine,
And be an ill foreboder?
I'm twenty-three, and five feet nine,
I'll go and be a sodger!

I gat some gear wi' mickle care,
I held it weel thegither;
But now it's gane, and something mair –
I'll go and be a sodger!

Song – No Churchman am I

No churchman am I for to rail and to write,
No statesman nor soldier to plot or to fight,
No sly man of business contriving a snare,
For a big-belly'd bottle's the whole of my care.

The peer I don't envy, I give him his bow;
I scorn not the peasant, though ever so low;
But a club of good fellows, like those that are here,
And a bottle like this, are my glory and care.
Here passes the squire on his brother – his horse;
There centum per centum, the cit with his purse;
But see you the Crown how it waves in the air?
There a big-belly'd bottle still eases my care.

The wife of my bosom, alas! she did die;
For sweet consolation to church I did fly;
I found that old Solomon proved it fair,
That a big-belly'd bottle's a cure for all care.

I once was persuaded a venture to make;
A letter inform'd me that all was to wreck;
But the pursy old landlord just waddl'd upstairs,
With a glorious bottle that ended my cares.

'Life's cares they are comforts' – a maxim laid down
By the Bard, what d'ye call him, that wore the black gown;
And faith I agree with th' old prig to a hair,
For a big-belly'd bottle's a heav'n of a care.

Song Composed in August
(1783)

Now westlin winds and slaught'ring guns
Bring Autumn's pleasant weather;
The moorcock springs on whirring wings
Amang the blooming heather:
Now waving grain, wide o'er the plain,
Delights the weary farmer;
And the moon shines bright, when I rove at night,
To muse upon my charmer.

The partridge loves the fruitful fells,
The plover loves the mountains;
The woodcock haunts the lonely dells,
The soaring hern the fountains:
Thro' lofty groves the cushat roves,
The path of man to shun it;
The hazel bush o'erhangs the thrush,
The spreading thorn the linnet.

Thus ev'ry kind their pleasure find,
The savage and the tender;
Some social join, and leagues combine,
Some solitary wander:

Avaunt, away! the cruel sway,
Tyrannic man's dominion;
The sportsman's joy, the murd'ring cry,
The flutt'ring, gory pinion!

But, Peggy dear, the ev'ning's clear,
Thick flies the skimming swallow,
The sky is blue, the fields in view,
All fading-green and yellow:
Come let us stray our gladsome way,
And view the charms of Nature;
The rustling corn, the fruited thorn,
And ev'ry happy creature.

We'll gently walk, and sweetly talk,
Till the silent moon shine clearly;
I'll grasp thy waist, and, fondly prest,
Swear how I love thee dearly:
Not vernal show'rs to budding flow'rs,
Not Autumn to the farmer,
So dear can be as thou to me,
My fair, my lovely charmer!

Remorse: a Fragment
(1784)

Of all the numerous ills that hurt our peace,
That press the soul, or wring the mind with anguish,
Beyond comparison the worst are those
By our own folly, or our guilt brought on:
In ev'ry other circumstance, the mind
Has this to say, 'It was no deed of mine:'
But, when to all the evil of misfortune
This sting is added, 'Blame thy foolish self!'
Or worser far, the pangs of keen remorse,
The torturing, gnawing consciousness of guilt –
Of guilt, perhaps, when we've involved others,
The young, the innocent, who fondly lov'd us;
Nay more, that very love their cause of ruin!
O burning hell! in all thy store of torments
There's not a keener lash!
Lives there a man so firm, who, while his heart
Feels all the bitter horrors of his crime,
Can reason down its agonizing throbs;
And, after proper purpose of amendment,
Can firmly force his jarring thoughts to peace?
O happy, happy, enviable man!
O glorious magnanimity of soul!

Epitaph on My Ever Honoured Father

(1784)

O ye whose cheek the tear of pity stains,
Draw near with pious rev'rence, and attend!
Here lie the loving husband's dear remains,
The tender father, and the gen'rous friend;
The pitying heart that felt for human woe,
The dauntless heart that fear'd no human pride;
The friend of man – to vice alone a foe;
For 'ev'n his failings lean'd to virtue's side'.*

*Goldsmith – R.B.

One Night as I Did Wander
(1785)

One night as I did wander,
When corn begins to shoot,
I sat me down to ponder
Upon an auld tree root;
Auld Ayr ran by before me,
And bicker'd to the seas;
A cushat crooded o'er me,
That echoed through the braes . . .

Tho' Cruel Fate Should Bid Us Part
(1785)

Tho' cruel fate should bid us part,
Far as the pole and line,
Her dear idea round my heart,
Should tenderly entwine.
Tho' mountains rise, and deserts howl,
And oceans roar between;
Yet, dearer than my deathless soul,
I still would love my Jean . . .

Address To A Haggis
(1786)

Fair fa' your honest, sonsie face,
Great Chieftan o' the Puddin'-race!
Aboon them a' ye tak your place,
    Painch, tripe, or thairm:
Weel are ye wordy o' a grace
  As lang's my arm.

The groaning trencher there ye fill,
Your hurdies like a distant hill,
Your pin wad help to mend a mill
    In time o' need,
While thro' your pores the dews distil
  Like amber bead.

His knife see Rustic-labour dight,
An' cut you up wi' ready sleight,
Trenching your gushing entrails bright,
    Like ony ditch;
And then, O what a glorious sight,
  Warm-reekin', rich!

Then, horn for horn they stretch an' strive:
Deil tak the hindmost! on they drive,
Till a' their weel-swall'd kytes belyve
   Are bent like drums;
Then auld Guidman, maist like to rive,
   Bethankit hums.

Is there that owre his French *ragout*
Or *olio* that wad staw a sow,
Or *fricassee* wad make her spew
   Wi' perfect sconner,
Looks down wi' sneering, scornfu' view
   On sic a dinner?

Poor devil! see him owre his trash,
As feckles as a wither'd rash,
His spindle-shank a guid whip-lash,
   His nieve a nit;
Thro' bluidy flood or field to dash,
   O how unfit!

But mark the Rustic, haggis-fed,
The trembling earth resounds his tread,
Clap in his walie nieve a blade,
   He'll mak it whissle;
An' legs an' arms, an' heads will sned,
   Like taps o' thrissle.

Ye Pow'rs wha mak mankind your care,
An' dish them out their bill o' fare,
Auld Scotland wants nae skinking ware
   That jaups in luggies;
But, if ye wish her gratefu' pray'r,
   Gie her a Haggis!

Song: Green Grow The Rashes: A Fragment
(1783)

CHORUS – *Green grow the rashes, O;*
Green grow the rashes, O;
The sweetest hours that e'er I spend,
　　Are spent amang the lasses, O.

There's nought but care on ev'ry han',
　　In ev'ry hour that passes, O:
What signifies the life o' man,
　　An' 'twere na for the lasses, O?
　　　Green grow, &c.

The war'ly race may riches chase,
　　An' riches still may fly them, O;
An' tho' at last they catch them fast,
　　Their hearts can ne'er enjoy them, O.
　　　Green grow, &c.

But gie me a cannie hour at e'en,
　　My arms about my Dearie, O;
An' war'ly cares, an' war'ly men,
　　May a' gae tapsalteerie, O!
　　　Green grow, &c.

For you sae douse, ye sneer at this,
　　Ye're nought but senseless asses, O:
The wisest Man the warl' e'er saw,
　　He dearly lov'd the lasses, O.
　　　Green grow, &c.

Auld Nature swears, the lovely Dears
　　Her noblest work she classes, O:
Her prentice han' she try'd on man,
　　An' then she made the lasses, O.
　　　Green grow, &c.

To A Mouse, On Turning Her Up In Her Nest
With The Plough, November, 1785

Wee, sleekit, cow'rin, tim'rous beastie,
O, what a panic's in thy breastie!
Thou need na start awa sae hasty,
    Wi' bickering brattle!
I wad be laith to rin an' chase thee,
    Wi' murd'ring pattle!

I'm truly sorry Man's dominion,
Has broken Nature's social union,
An' justifies that ill opinion,
    Which makes thee startle
At me, thy poor, earth-born companion,
    An' fellow-mortal!

I doubt na, whiles, but thou may thieve;
What then? poor beastie, thou maun live!
A daimen icker in a thrave
    'S a sma' request;
I'll get a blessin wi' the lave,
    An' never miss't!

Thy wee bit housie, too, in ruin!
Its silly wa's the win's are strewin!
An' naething, now, to big a new ane,
    O' foggage green!
An' bleak December's winds ensuin,
    Baith snell an' keen!

Thou saw the fields laid bare an' wast,
An' weary winter comin fast,
An' cozie here, beneath the blast,
    Thou thought to dwell –
Till crash! the cruel coulter past
    Out thro' thy cell.

That wee-bit heap o' leaves an' stibble,
Has cost thee mony a weary nibble!
Now thou's turn'd out, for a' thy trouble,
    But house or hald,
To thole the winter's sleety dribble,
    An' cranreuch cauld!

But, Mousie, thou art no thy-lane,
In proving foresight may be vain;
The best-laid schemes o' mice an' men
    Gang aft agley,
An' lea'e us nought but grief an' pain,
    For promis'd joy!

Still thou art blest, compar'd wi' me!
The present only toucheth thee:
But, Och! I backward cast my e'e,
    On prospects drear!
An' forward, tho' I canna see,
    I guess an' fear!

To John Kennedy, Dumfries House

(1786)

Now, Kennedy, if foot or horse
E'er bring you in by Mauchlin corse,
(Lord, man, there's lasses there wad force
A hermit's fancy;
An' down the gate in faith they're worse,
An' mair unchancy).

But as I'm sayin, please step to Dow's,
An' taste sic gear as Johnie brews,
Till some bit callan bring me news
That ye are there;
An' if we dinna hae a bouze,
I'se ne'er drink mair.

It's no I like to sit an' swallow,
Then like a swine to puke an' wallow;
But gie me just a true good fallow,
Wi' right ingine,
And spunkie ance to mak us mellow,
An' then we'll shine.

Now if ye're ane o' warl's folk,
Wha rate the wearer by the cloak,
An' sklent on poverty their joke,
Wi' bitter sneer,
Wi' you nae friendship I will troke,
Nor cheap nor dear.

But if, as I'm informed weel,
Ye hate as ill's the very deil
The flinty heart that canna feel –
Come, sir, here's to you!
Hae, there's my haun', I wiss you weel,
An' gude be wi' you.

To a Mountain Daisy
On turning one down with the Plough,
in April, 1786

Wee, modest crimson-tipped flow'r,
Thou's met me in an evil hour;
For I maun crush amang the stoure
Thy slender stem:
To spare thee now is past my pow'r,
Thou bonie gem.

Alas! it's no thy neibor sweet,
The bonie lark, companion meet,
Bending thee 'mang the dewy weet,
Wi' spreckl'd breast!
When upward-springing, blythe, to greet
The purpling east.

Cauld blew the bitter-biting north
Upon thy early, humble birth;
Yet cheerfully thou glinted forth
Amid the storm,
Scarce rear'd above the parent-earth
Thy tender form.

The flaunting flow'rs our gardens yield,
High shelt'ring woods and wa's maun shield;
But thou, beneath the random bield
O' clod or stane,
Adorns the histie stibble field,
Unseen, alane.

There, in thy scanty mantle clad,
Thy snawie bosom sun-ward spread,
Thou lifts thy unassuming head
In humble guise;
But now the share uptears thy bed,
And low thou lies!

Such is the fate of artless maid,
Sweet flow'ret of the rural shade!
By love's simplicity betray'd,
And guileless trust;
Till she, like thee, all soil'd, is laid
Low i' the dust.

Such is the fate of simple bard,
On life's rough ocean luckless starr'd!
Unskilful he to note the card
Of prudent lore,
Till billows rage, and gales blow hard,
And whelm him o'er!

Such fate to suffering worth is giv'n,
Who long with wants and woes has striv'n,
By human pride or cunning driv'n
To mis'ry's brink;
Till wrench'd of ev'ry stay but Heav'n,
He, ruin'd, sink!

Ev'n thou who mourn'st the Daisy's fate,
That fate is thine – no distant date;
Stern Ruin's plough-share drives elate,
Full on thy bloom,
Till crush'd beneath the furrow's weight,
Shall be thy doom!

To Ruin

(1786)

All hail! inexorable lord!
At whose destruction-breathing word,
The mightiest empires fall!
Thy cruel, woe-delighted train,
The ministers of grief and pain,
A sullen welcome, all!

With stern-resolv'd, despairing eye,
I see each aimed dart;
For one has cut my dearest tie,
And quivers in my heart.
Then low'ring, and pouring,
The storm no more I dread;
Tho' thick'ning, and black'ning,
Round my devoted head.

And thou grim Pow'r by life abhorr'd,
While life a pleasure can afford,
Oh! hear a wretch's pray'r!
Nor more I shrink appall'd, afraid;
I court, I beg thy friendly aid,
To close this scene of care!

When shall my soul, in silent peace,
Resign life's joyless day –
My weary heart its throbbing cease,
Cold mould'ring in the clay?
No fear more, no tear more,
To stain my lifeless face,
Enclasped, and grasped,
Within thy cold embrace!

Song – Will Ye Go To The Indies, My Mary?
(1786)

Will ye go to the Indies, my Mary,
And leave auld Scotia's shore?
Will ye go to the Indies, my Mary,
Across th' Atlantic roar?

O sweet grows the lime and the orange,
And the apple on the pine;
But a' the charms o' the Indies
Can never equal thine.

I hae sworn by the Heavens to my Mary,
I hae sworn by the Heavens to be true;
And sae may the Heavens forget me,
When I forget my vow!

O plight me your faith, my Mary,
And plight me your lily-white hand;
O plight me your faith, my Mary,
Before I leave Scotia's strand.

We hae plighted our troth, my Mary,
In mutual affection to join;
And curst be the cause that shall part us!
The hour and the moment o' time!

Lines Written on a Banknote

(1786)

Wae worth thy power, thou cursed leaf!
Fell source o' a' my woe and grief!
For lack o' thee I've lost my lass!
For lack o' thee I scrimp my glass!
I see the children of affliction
Unaided, through thy curst restriction:
I've seen the oppressor's cruel smile
Amid his hapless victim's spoil;
And for thy potence vainly wished,
To crush the villain in the dust:
For lack o' thee, I leave this much-lov'd shore,
Never, perhaps, to greet old Scotland more.

Nature's Law – a Poem (1786)
Humbly inscribed to Gavin Hamilton, Esq.

Great Nature spoke: observant man obey'd – POPE

Let other heroes boast their scars,
The marks of sturt and strife:
And other poets sing of wars,
The plagues of human life:

Shame fa' the fun, wi' sword and gun
To slap mankind like lumber!
I sing his name, and nobler fame,
Wha multiplies our number.

Great Nature spoke, with air benign,
'Go on, ye human race;
This lower world I you resign;
Be fruitful and increase.
The liquid fire of strong desire
I've pour'd it in each bosom;
Here, on this hand, does Mankind stand,
And there is Beauty's blossom.'

The Hero of these artless strains,
A lowly bard was he,
Who sung his rhymes in Coila's plains,
With meikle mirth an' glee;
Kind Nature's care had given his share
Large, of the flaming current;
And, all devout, he never sought
To stem the sacred torrent.

He felt the powerful, high behest
Thrill, vital, thro' and thro';
And sought a correspondent breast,
To give obedience due:
Propitious Powers screen'd the young flow'rs,
From mildews of abortion;
And lo! the bard – a great reward –
Has got a double portion!

Auld cantie Coil may count the day,
As annual it returns,
The third of Libra's equal sway,
That gave another Burns,
With future rhymes, an' other times,
To emulate his sire:
To sing auld Coil in nobler style
With more poetic fire.

Ye Powers of peace, and peaceful song,
Look down with gracious eyes;
And bless auld Coila, large and long,
With multiplying joys;
Lang may she stand to prop the land,
The flow'r of ancient nations;
And Burnses spring, her fame to sing,
To endless generations!

Song – Bonie Dundee

(1787)

My blessin's upon thy sweet wee lippie!
My blessin's upon thy e'e-brie!
Thy smiles are sae like my blythe sodger laddie,
Thou's aye the dearer, and dearer to me!

But I'll big a bow'r on yon bonie banks,
Whare Tay rins wimplin' by sae clear;
An' I'll cleed thee in the tartan sae fine,
And mak thee a man like thy daddie dear.

The Book-Worms

(1787)

Through and through th' inspir'd leaves,
Ye maggots, make your windings;
But O respect his lordship's taste,
And spare his golden bindings.

On Elphinstone's Translation
of Martial's Epigrams
(1787)

O Thou whom Poetry abhors,
Whom Prose has turned out of doors,
Heard'st thou yon groan?– proceed no further,
'Twas laurel'd Martial calling murther.

The Libeller's Self-Reproof
(1787)

Rash mortal, and slanderous poet, thy name
Shall no longer appear in the records of Fame;
Dost not know that old Mansfield, who writes like the Bible,
Says, the more 'tis a truth, sir, the more 'tis a libel!

Song – A Bottle and Friend
(1787)

'There's nane that's blest of human kind,
But the cheerful and the gay, man,
Fal, la, la,' &c.

Here's a bottle and an honest friend!
What wad ye wish for mair, man?
Wha kens, before his life may end,
What his share may be o' care, man?

Then catch the moments as they fly,
And use them as ye ought, man:
Believe me, happiness is shy,
And comes not aye when sought, man.

Castle Gordon
(1787)

Streams that glide in orient plains,
Never bound by Winter's chains;
Glowing here on golden sands,
There immix'd with foulest stains
From Tyranny's empurpled hands;
These, their richly gleaming waves,
I leave to tyrants and their slaves;
Give me the stream that sweetly laves
The banks by Castle Gordon.

Spicy forests, ever gray,
Shading from the burning ray
Hapless wretches sold to toil;
Or the ruthless native's way,
Bent on slaughter, blood, and spoil:
Woods that ever verdant wave,
I leave the tyrant and the slave;
Give me the groves that lofty brave
The storms by Castle Gordon.

Wildly here, without control,
Nature reigns and rules the whole;
In that sober pensive mood,
Dearest to the feeling soul,
She plants the forest, pours the flood:
Life's poor day I'll musing rave
And find at night a sheltering cave,
Where waters flow and wild woods wave,
By bonie Castle Gordon.

On Scaring Some Water-Fowl in Loch-Turit
A wild scene among the Hills of Oughtertyre
(1787)

Why, ye tenants of the lake,
For me your wat'ry haunt forsake?
Tell me, fellow-creatures, why
At my presence thus you fly?
Why disturb your social joys,
Parent, filial, kindred ties? –

Common friend to you and me,
Nature's gifts to all are free:
Peaceful keep your dimpling wave,
Busy feed, or wanton lave;
Or, beneath the sheltering rock,
Bide the surging billow's shock.

Conscious, blushing for our race,
Soon, too soon, your fears I trace,
Man, your proud, usurping foe,
Would be lord of all below:
Plumes himself in freedom's pride,
Tyrant stern to all beside.

The eagle, from the cliffy brow,
Marking you his prey below,
In his breast no pity dwells,
Strong necessity compels:
But Man, to whom alone is giv'n
A ray direct from pitying Heav'n,
Glories in his heart humane –
And creatures for his pleasure slain!

In these savage, liquid plains,
Only known to wand'ring swains,
Where the mossy riv'let strays,
Far from human haunts and ways;
All on Nature you depend,
And life's poor season peaceful spend.

Or, if man's superior might
Dare invade your native right,
On the lofty ether borne,
Man with all his pow'rs you scorn;
Swiftly seek, on clanging wings,
Other lakes and other springs;
And the foe you cannot brave,
Scorn at least to be his slave.

A Rose-Bud By My Early Walk

(1787)

A Rose-bud by my early walk,
Adown a corn-enclosed bawk,
Sae gently bent its thorny stalk,
All on a dewy morning.
Ere twice the shades o' dawn are fled,
In a' its crimson glory spread,
And drooping rich the dewy head,
It scents the early morning.

Within the bush her covert nest
A little linnet fondly prest;
The dew sat chilly on her breast,
Sae early in the morning.
She soon shall see her tender brood,
The pride, the pleasure o' the wood,
Amang the fresh green leaves bedew'd,
Awake the early morning.

So thou, dear bird, young Jeany fair,
On trembling string or vocal air,
Shall sweetly pay the tender care
That tents thy early morning.
So thou, sweet Rose-bud, young and gay,
Shalt beauteous blaze upon the day,
And bless the parent's evening ray
That watch'd thy early morning.

My Peggy's Charms

(1787)

My Peggy's face, my Peggy's form,
The frost of hermit Age might warm;
My Peggy's worth, my Peggy's mind,
Might charm the first of human kind.

I love my Peggy's angel air,
Her face so truly heavenly fair,
Her native grace, so void of art,
But I adore my Peggy's heart.

The lily's hue, the rose's dye,
The kindling lustre of an eye;
Who but owns their magic sway!
Who but knows they all decay!

The tender thrill, the pitying tear,
The generous purpose nobly dear,
The gentle look that rage disarms –
These are all Immortal charms.

Love in the Guise of Friendship

(1788)

Your friendship much can make me blest,
O why that bliss destroy!
Why urge the only, one request
You know I will deny!

Your thought, if Love must harbour there,
Conceal it in that thought;
Nor cause me from my bosom tear
The very friend I sought.

I'm O'er Young to Marry Yet
(1788)

Chorus. – *I'm o'er young, I'm o'er young,*
I'm o'er young to marry yet;
I'm o'er young, 'twad be a sin
To tak me frae my mammy yet.

I am my mammny's ae bairn,
Wi' unco folk I weary, sir;
And lying in a man's bed,
I'm fley'd it mak me eerie, sir.
I'm o'er young, &c.

My mammie coft me a new gown,
The kirk maun hae the gracing o't;
Were I to lie wi' you, kind Sir,
I'm feared ye'd spoil the lacing o't.
I'm o'er young, &c.

Hallowmass is come and gane,
The nights are lang in winter, sir,
And you an' I in ae bed,
In trowth, I dare na venture, sir.
I'm o'er young, &c.

[52]

Fu' loud an' shill the frosty wind
Blaws thro' the leafless timmer, sir;
But if ye come this gate again;
I'll aulder be gin simmer, sir.
I'm o'er young, &c.

M'Pherson's Farewell
(1788)

Farewell, ye dungeons dark and strong,
The wretch's destinie!
M'Pherson's time will not be long
On yonder gallows-tree.

Chorus. – *Sae rantingly, sae wantonly,*
Sae dauntingly gaed he;
He play'd a spring, and danc'd it round,
Below the gallows-tree.

O, what is death but parting breath?
On many a bloody plain
I've dared his face, and in this place
I scorn him yet again!
Sae rantingly, &c.

Untie these bands from off my hands,
And bring me to my sword;
And there's no a man in all Scotland
But I'll brave him at a word.
Sae rantingly, &c.

I've liv'd a life of sturt and strife;
I die by treacherie:
It burns my heart I must depart,
And not avengèd be.
Sae rantingly, &c.

Now farewell light, thou sunshine bright,
And all beneath the sky!
May coward shame distain his name,
The wretch that dares not die!
Sae rantingly, &c.

To Alex. Cunningham, Esq., Writer
Ellisland, Nithsdale, July 27th, 1788

My godlike friend – nay, do not stare,
You think the phrase is odd-like;
But God is love, the saints declare,
Then surely thou art god-like.

And is thy ardour still the same?
And kindled still at Anna?
Others may boast a partial flame,
But thou art a volcano!

Ev'n Wedlock asks not love beyond
Death's tie-dissolving portal;
But thou, omnipotently fond,
May'st promise love immortal!

Thy wounds such healing powers defy,
Such symptoms dire attend them,
That last great antihectic try –
Marriage perhaps may mend them.

Sweet Anna has an air – a grace,
Divine, magnetic, touching:
She talks, she charms – but who can trace
The process of bewitching?

Song – The Day Returns
(1788)

The day returns, my bosom burns,
The blissful day we twa did meet:
Tho' winter wild in tempest toil'd,
Ne'er summer-sun was half sae sweet.
Than a' the pride that loads the tide,
And crosses o'er the sultry line;
Than kingly robes, than crowns and globes,
Heav'n gave me more – it made thee mine!

While day and night can bring delight,
Or Nature aught of pleasure give;
While joys above my mind can move,
For thee, and thee alone, I live.
When that grim foe of life below
Comes in between to make us part,
The iron hand that breaks our band,
It breaks my bliss – it breaks my heart!

A Mother's Lament
For the Death of Her Son
(1788)

Fate gave the word, the arrow sped,
And pierc'd my darling's heart;
And with him all the joys are fled
Life can to me impart.

By cruel hands the sapling drops,
In dust dishonour'd laid;
So fell the pride of all my hopes,
My age's future shade.

The mother-linnet in the brake
Bewails her ravish'd young;
So I, for my lost darling's sake,
Lament the live-day long.

Death, oft I've feared thy fatal blow.
Now, fond, I bare my breast;
O, do thou kindly lay me low
With him I love, at rest!

The Fall of the Leaf

(1788)

The lazy mist hangs from the brow of the hill,
Concealing the course of the dark-winding rill;
How languid the scenes, late so sprightly, appear!
As Autumn to Winter resigns the pale year.

The forests are leafless, the meadows are brown,
And all the gay foppery of summer is flown:
Apart let me wander, apart let me muse,
How quick Time is flying, how keen Fate pursues!

How long I have liv'd – but how much liv'd in vain,
How little of life's scanty span may remain,
What aspects old Time in his progress has worn,
What ties cruel Fate, in my bosom has torn.

How foolish, or worse, till our summit is gain'd!
And downward, how weaken'd, how darken'd, how pain'd!
Life is not worth having with all it can give –
For something beyond it poor man sure must live.

My Bonie Mary

(1788)

Go, fetch to me a pint o' wine,
And fill it in a silver tassie;
That I may drink before I go,
A service to my bonie lassie.
The boat rocks at the pier o' Leith;
Fu' loud the wind blaws frae the Ferry;
The ship rides by the Berwick-law,
And I maun leave my bonie Mary.

The trumpets sound, the banners fly,
The glittering spears are ranked ready:
The shouts o' war are heard afar,
The battle closes deep and bloody;
It's not the roar o' sea or shore,
Wad mak me langer wish to tarry!
Nor shouts o' war that's heard afar –
It's leaving thee, my bonie Mary!

Written In Friars Carse Hermitage
On Nithside

(1788)

Thou whom chance may hither lead,
Be thou clad in russet weed,
Be thou deckt in silken stole,
Grave these counsels on thy soul.

Life is but a day at most,
Sprung from night, – in darkness lost;
Hope not sunshine ev'ry hour,
Fear not clouds will always lour.

As Youth and Love with sprightly dance,
Beneath thy morning star advance,
Pleasure with her siren air
May delude the thoughtless pair;
Let Prudence bless Enjoyment's cup,
Then raptur'd sip, and sip it up.

As thy day grows warm and high,
Life's meridian flaming nigh,
Dost thou spurn the humble vale?
Life's proud summits wouldst thou scale?

Check thy climbing step, elate,
Evils lurk in felon wait:
Dangers, eagle-pinioned, bold,
Soar around each cliffy hold!
While cheerful Peace, with linnet song,
Chants the lowly dells among.

As the shades of ev'ning close,
Beck'ning thee to long repose;
As life itself becomes disease,
Seek the chimney-nook of ease;
There ruminate with sober thought,
On all thou'st seen, and heard, and wrought,
And teach the sportive younkers round,
Saws of experience, sage and sound:
Say, man's true, genuine estimate,
The grand criterion of his fate,
Is not, – Art thou high or low?
Did thy fortune ebb or flow?
Did many talents gild thy span?
Or frugal Nature grudge thee one?
Tell them, and press it on their mind,
As thou thyself must shortly find,
The smile or frown of awful Heav'n,
To virtue or to Vice is giv'n,

Say, to be just, and kind, and wise –
There solid self-enjoyment lies;
That foolish, selfish, faithless ways
Lead to be wretched, vile, and base.

Thus resign'd and quiet, creep
To the bed of lasting sleep, –
Sleep, whence thou shalt ne'er awake,
Night, where dawn shall never break,
Till future life, future no more,
To light and joy the good restore,
To light and joy unknown before.
Stranger, go! Heav'n be thy guide!
Quod the Beadsman of Nithside.

Caledonia – a Ballad

(1789)

There was once a day, but old Time was then young,
That brave Caledonia, the chief of her line,
From some of your northern deities sprung,
(Who knows not that brave Caledonia's divine?)
From Tweed to the Orcades was her domain,
To hunt, or to pasture, or do what she would:
Her heav'nly relations there fixed her reign,
And pledg'd her their godheads to warrant it good.

A lambkin in peace, but a lion in war,
The pride of her kindred, the heroine grew:
Her grandsire, old Odin, triumphantly swore, –
'Whoe'er shall provoke thee, th' encounter shall rue!'
With tillage or pasture at times she would sport,
To feed her fair flocks by her green rustling corn;
But chiefly the woods were her fav'rite resort,
Her darling amusement, the hounds and the horn.

Long quiet she reigned; till thitherward steers
A flight of bold eagles from Adria's strand:
Repeated, successive, for many long years,
They darken'd the air, and they plunder'd the land:
Their pounces were murder, and terror their cry,
They'd conquer'd and ruin'd a world beside;
She took to her hills, and her arrows let fly,
The daring invaders they fled or they died.

The Cameleon-Savage disturb'd her repose,
With tumult, disquiet, rebellion, and strife;
Provok'd beyond bearing, at last she arose,
And robb'd him at once of his hopes and his life:
The Anglian lion, the terror of France,
Oft prowling, ensanguin'd the Tweed's silver flood;
But, taught by the bright Caledonian lance,
He learned to fear in his own native wood.

The fell Harpy-raven took wing from the north,
The scourge of the seas, and the dread of the shore;
The wild Scandinavian boar issued forth
To wanton in carnage and wallow in gore:
O'er countries and kingdoms their fury prevail'd,
No arts could appease them, no arms could repel;
But brave Caledonia in vain they assail'd,
As Largs well can witness, and Loncartie tell.

Thus bold, independent, unconquer'd, and free,
Her bright course of glory for ever shall run:
For brave Caledonia immortal must be;
I'll prove it from Euclid as clear as the sun:
Rectangle-triangle, the figure we'll chuse:
The upright is Chance, and old Time is the base;
But brave Caledonia's the hypothenuse;
Then, ergo, she'll match them, and match them always.

The Wounded Hare

(1789)

Inhuman man! curse on thy barb'rous art,
And blasted be thy murder-aiming eye;
May never pity soothe thee with a sigh,
Nor ever pleasure glad thy cruel heart!

Go live, poor wand'rer of the wood and field!
The bitter little that of life remains:
No more the thickening brakes and verdant plains
To thee a home, or food, or pastime yield.

Seek, mangled wretch, some place of wonted rest,
No more of rest, but now thy dying bed!
The sheltering rushes whistling o'er thy head,
The cold earth with thy bloody bosom prest.

Perhaps a mother's anguish adds its woe;
The playful pair crowd fondly by thy side;
Ah! helpless nurslings, who will now provide
That life a mother only can bestow!

Oft as by winding Nith I, musing, wait
The sober eve, or hail the cheerful dawn,
I'll miss thee sporting o'er the dewy lawn,
And curse the ruffian's aim, and mourn thy hapless fate.

On a Bank of Flowers

(1789)

On a bank of flowers, in a summer day,
For summer lightly drest,
The youthful, blooming Nelly lay,
With love and sleep opprest;
When Willie, wand'ring thro' the wood,
Who for her favour oft had sued;
He gaz'd, he wish'd
He fear'd, he blush'd,
And trembled where he stood.

Her closed eyes, like weapons sheath'd,
Were seal'd in soft repose;
Her lip, still as she fragrant breath'd,
It richer dyed the rose;
The springing lilies, sweetly prest,
Wild-wanton kissed her rival breast;
He gaz'd, he wish'd,
He mear'd, he blush'd,
His bosom ill at rest.

Her robes, light-waving in the breeze,
Her tender limbs embrace;
Her lovely form, her native ease,
All harmony and grace;
Tumultuous tides his pulses roll,
A faltering, ardent kiss he stole;
He gaz'd, he wish'd,
He fear'd, he blush'd,
And sigh'd his very soul.

As flies the partridge from the brake,
On fear-inspired wings,
So Nelly, starting, half-awake,
Away affrighted springs;
But Willie follow'd – as he should,
He overtook her in the wood;
He vow'd, he pray'd,
He found the maid
Forgiving all, and good.

The Braes o' Killiecrankie

(1789)

Where hae ye been sae braw, lad?
Whare hae ye been sae brankie, O?
Whare hae ye been sae braw, lad?
Cam ye by Killiecrankie, O?

Chorus – *An ye had been whare I hae been,*
Ye wad na been sae cantie, O;
An ye had seen what I hae seen,
I' the Braes o' Killiecrankie, O.

I faught at land, I faught at sea,
At hame I faught my Auntie, O;
But I met the devil an' Dundee,
On the Braes o' Killiecrankie, O.
An ye had been, &c.

The bauld Pitcur fell in a furr,
An' Clavers gat a clankie, O;
Or I had fed an Athole gled,
On the Braes o' Killiecrankie, O.
An ye had been, &c.

The Banks of Nith

(1789)

The Thames flows proudly to the sea,
Where royal cities stately stand;
But sweeter flows the Nith to me,
Where Comyns ance had high command.
When shall I see that honour'd land,
That winding stream I love so dear!
Must wayward Fortune's adverse hand
For ever, ever keep me here!

How lovely, Nith, thy fruitful vales,
Where bounding hawthorns gaily bloom;
And sweetly spread thy sloping dales,
Where lambkins wanton through the broom.
Tho' wandering now must be my doom,
Far from thy bonie banks and braes,
May there my latest hours consume,
Amang the friends of early days!

Tam O' Shanter: A Tale

(1790)

Of Brownyis and of Bogillis full is this Buke.
GAWIN DOUGLAS

When chapman billies leave the street,
And drouthy neibors, neibors, meet;
As market days are wearing late,
An' folk begin to tak the gate,
While we sit bousing at the nappy,
An' getting fou and unco happy,
We think na on the lang Scots miles,
The mosses, waters, slaps and stiles,
That lie between us and our hame,
Where sits our sulky sullen dame,
Gathering her brows like gathering storm,
Nursing her wrath to keep it warm.

This truth fand honest Tam o' Shanter,
As he frae Ayr ae night did canter:
(Auld Ayr, wham ne'er a town surpasses,
For honest men and bonie lasses).

O Tam! had'st thou but been sae wise,
As taen thy ain wife Kate's advice!
She tauld thee weel thou was a skellum,
A blethering, blustering, drunken blellum;
That frae November till October,
Ae market-day thou was nae sober;
That ilka melder wi' the Miller,
Thou sat as lang as thou had siller;
That ev'ry naig was ca'd a shoe on
The smith and thee gat roarin' fou on;
That at the Lord's house, ev'n on Sunday,
Thou drank wi' Kirkton Jean till Monday,
She prophesied that late or soon,
Thou wad be found, deep drown'd in Doon,
Or catch'd wi' warlocks in the mirk,
By Alloway's auld, haunted kirk.

Ah, gentle dames! it gars me greet,
To think how mony counsels sweet,
How mony lengthen'd, sage advices,
The husband frae the wife despises!

But to our tale: Ae market night,
Tam had got planted unco right,
Fast by an ingle, bleezing finely,
Wi' reaming swats, that drank divinely;
And at his elbow, Souter Johnie,
His ancient, trusty, drouthy crony:
Tam lo'ed him like a very brither;
They had been fou for weeks thegither.
The night drave on wi' sangs an' clatter;
And aye the ale was growing better:
The landlady and Tam grew gracious,
Wi' favours secret, sweet, and precious:
The Souter tauld his queerest stories;
The landlord's laugh was ready chorus:
The storm without might rair and rustle,
Tam did na mind the storm a whistle.

Care, mad to see a man sae happy,
E'en drown'd himsel' amang the nappy.
As bees flee hame wi' lades o' treasure,
The minutes wing'd their way wi' pleasure:
Kings may be blest, but Tam was glorious,
O'er a' the ills o' life victorious!

But pleasures are like poppies spread,
You seize the flow'r, its bloom is shed;
Or like the snow falls in the river,
A moment white – then melts for ever;
Or like the borealis race,
That flit ere you can point their place;
Or like the rainbow's lovely form
Evanishing amid the storm. –
Nae man can tether time nor tide,
The hour approaches Tam maun ride;
That hour, o' night's black arch the key-stane,
That dreary hour he mounts his beast in;
And sic a night he taks the road in,
As ne'er poor sinner was abroad in.

The wind blew as 'twad blawn its last;
The rattling showers rose on the blast;
The speedy gleams the darkness swallow'd;
Loud, deep, and lang, the thunder bellow'd:
That night, a child might understand,
The Deil had business on his hand.

Weel-mounted on his grey mare, Meg,
A better never lifted leg,
Tam skelpit on thro' dub and mire,
Despising wind, and rain, and fire;
Whiles holding fast his gude blue bonnet,
Whiles crooning o'er some auld Scots sonnet,
Whiles glow'rin round wi' prudent cares,
Lest bogles catch him unawares;
Kirk-Alloway was drawing nigh,
Where ghaists and houlets nightly cry.

By this time he was cross the ford,
Whare in the snaw the chapman smoor'd;
And past the birks and meikle stane,
Whare drunken Charlie brak's neck-bane;
And thro' the whins, and by the cairn,
Whare hunters fand the murder'd bairn;
And near the thorn, aboon the well,
Whare Mungo's mither hang'd hersel'.

Before him Doon pours all his floods,
The doubling storm roars thro' the woods,
The lightnings flash from pole to pole,
Near and more near the thunders roll,
When, glimmering thro' the groaning trees,
Kirk-Alloway seem'd in a bleeze,
Thro' ilka bore the beams were glancing,
And loud resounded mirth and dancing.

Inspiring bold John Barleycorn!
What dangers thou canst make us scorn!
Wi' tippenny, we fear nae evil;
Wi' usquabae, we'll face the devil!
The swats sae ream'd in Tammie's noddle,
Fair play, he car'd na deils a boddle,
But Maggie stood, right sair astonish'd,
Till, by the heel and hand admonish'd,
She ventur'd forward on the light;
And, vow! Tam saw an unco sight!

Warlocks and witches in a dance:
Nae cotillion, brent-new frae France,
But hornpipes, jigs, strathspeys, and reels,
Put life and mettle in their heels.

A winnock-bunker in the east,
There sat auld Nick, in shape o' beast;
A towzie tyke, black, grim, and large,
To gie them music was his charge:
He screw'd the pipes and gart them skirl,
Till roof and rafters a' did dirl. –
Coffins stood round, like open presses,
That shaw'd the Dead in their last dresses;
And, by some devilish cantraip sleight,
Each in its cauld hand held a light. –
By which heroic Tam was able
To note upon the haly table,
A murderer's banes, in gibbet-airns;
Twa span-lang, wee, unchristen'd bairns;
A thief, new-cutted frae a rape,
Wi' his last gasp his gab did gape;
Five tomahawks, wi' blude red-rusted:
Five scymitars, wi' murder crusted;
A garter which a babe had strangled:
A knife, a father's throat had mangled,
Whom his ain son of life bereft,
The grey-hairs yet stack to the heft;
Wi' mair of horrible an' awefu',
Which ev'n to name wad be unlawfu'.

As Tammie glowr'd, amaz'd, and curious,
The mirth and fun grew fast and furious;
The piper loud and louder blew,
The dancers quick and quicker flew,
The reel'd, they set, they cross'd, they cleekit,
Till ilka carlin swat and reekit,
And coost her duddies to the wark,
And linkit at it in her sark!

Now Tam, O Tam! had they been queans,
A' plump and strapping in their teens!
Their sarks, instead o' creeshie flannen,
Been snaw-white seventeen hunder linen! –
Thir breeks o' mine, my only pair,
That ance were plush o' guid blue hair,
I wad hae gi'en them off my hurdies,
For ae blink o' the bonie burdies!
But wither'd beldams, auld and droll,
Rigwoodie hags wad spean a foal,
Louping an' flinging on a crummock.
I wonder did na turn thy stomach.

But Tam kend what was what fu' brawlie:
There was ae winsome wench and wawlie
That night enlisted in the core,
Lang after kend on Carrick shore;
(For mony a beast to dead she shot,
And perish'd mony a bonie boat,
And shook baith meikle corn and bear,
And kept the country-side in fear);
Her cutty sark, o' Paisley harn,
That while a lassie she had worn,
In longitude tho' sorely scanty,
It was her best, and she was vauntie.
Ah! little kend thy reverend grannie,
That sark she coft for her wee Nannie,
Wi' twa pund Scots ('twas a' her riches),
Wad ever grac'd a dance o' witches!

But here my Muse her wing maun cour,
Sic flights are far beyond her power;
To sing how Nannie lap and flang,
(A souple jade she was and strang),
And how Tam stood, like ane bewitch'd,
And thought his very een enrich'd:
Even Satan glowr'd, and fidg'd fu' fain,
And hotch'd and blew wi' might and main:

Till first ae caper, syne anither,
Tam tint his reason a' thegither,
And roars out, 'Weel done, Cutty-sark!'
And in an instant all was dark:
And scarcely had he Maggie rallied,
When out the hellish legion sallied.

As bees bizz out wi' angry fyke,
When plundering herds assail their byke;
As open pussie's mortal foes,
When, pop! she starts before their nose;
As eager runs the market-crowd,
When 'Catch the thief!' resounds aloud;
So Maggie runs, the witches follow,
Wi' mony an eldritch skriech and hollow.

Ah, Tam! Ah, Tam! thou'll get thy fairin!
In hell, they'll roast thee like a herrin!
In vain thy Kate awaits thy comin!
Kate soon will be a woefu' woman!
Now, do thy speedy utmost, Meg,
And win the key-stane o' the brig;*
There, at them thou thy tail may toss,
A running stream they dare na cross.
But ere the key-stane she could make,

The fient a tail she had to shake!
For Nannie, far before the rest,
Hard upon noble Maggie prest,
And flew at Tam wi' furious ettle;
But little wist she Maggie's mettle!
Ae spring brought off her master hale,
But left behind her ain grey tail:
The carlin claught her by the rump,
And left poor Maggie scarce a stump.

Now, wha this tale o' truth shall read,
Ilk man and mother's son, take heed:
Whene'er to drink you are inclin'd,
Or cutty-sarks rin in your mind,
Think, ye may buy the joys o'er dear:
Remember Tam o' Shanter's mare.

---

* 'It is a well-known fact that witches, *or any evil spirits*, have *no* power to follow a poor *wight* any further than the middle of the next running stream. It may be proper likewise to mention to the benighted traveller, that when he falls in with bogles, whatever danger may be in his going forward, there is much more hazard in turning back.' – RB

John Barleycorn: A Ballad
(1782)

There was three kings into the east,
　　Three kings both great and high,
And they hae sworn a solemn oath
　　John Barleycorn should die.

They took a plough and plough'd him down,
　　Put clods upon his head,
And they hae sworn a solemn oath
　　John Barleycorn was dead.

But the cheerful spring came kindly on,
　　And show'rs began to fall;
John Barleycorn got up again,
　　And sore surpris'd them all.

The sultry suns of summer came,
　　And he grew thick and strong;
His head weel arm'd wi' pointed spears,
　　That no one should him wrong.

The sober autumn enter'd mild,
    When he grew wan and pale;
His bending joints and drooping head
    Show'd he began to fail.

His colour sicken'd more and more,
    He faded into age;
And then his enemies began
    To show their deadly rage.

They've taen a weapon, long and sharp,
    And cut him by the knee;
Then ty'd him fast upon a cart,
    Like a rogue for forgerie.

They laid him down upon his back,
    And cudgell'd him full sore;
They hung him up before the storm,
    And turned him o'er and o'er.

They filled up a darksome pit
    With water to the brim;
They heaved in John Barleycorn,
    There let him sink or swim.

They laid him out upon the floor,
  To work him farther woe;
And still, as signs of life appear'd,
  They toss'd him to and fro.

They wasted, o'er a scorching flame,
  The marrow of his bones;
But a miller us'd him worst of all,
  For he crush'd him between two stones.

And they hae taen his very heart's blood,
  And drank it round and round;
And still the more and more they drank,
  Their joy did more abound.

John Barleycorn was a hero bold,
  Of noble enterprise;
For if you do but taste his blood,
  'Twill make your courage rise.

'Twill make a man forget his woe;
  'Twill heighten all his joy;
'Twill make the widow's heart to sing,
  Tho' the tear were in her eye.

Then let us toast John Barleycorn,
 Each man a glass in hand;
And may his great posterity
 Ne'er fail in old Scotland!

The Twa Dogs: A Tale
(1786)

'Twas in that place o' Scotland's isle,
That bears the name o' auld King Coil,
Upon a bonie day in June,
When wearin' thro' the afternoon,
Twa dogs, that were na thrang at hame,
Forgather'd ance upon a time.

The first I'll name, they ca'd him Caesar,
Was keepit for His Honour's pleasure:
His hair, his size, his mouth, his lugs,
Shew'd he was nane o' Scotland's dogs;
But whalpit some place far abroad,
Whare sailors gang to fish for cod.
His locked, letter'd, braw brass collar
Shew'd him the gentleman an' scholar;

But though he was o' high degree,
The fient a pride, nae pride had he;
But wad hae spent an hour caressin,
Ev'n wi' al tinkler-gipsy's messin:
At kirk or market, mill or smiddie,
Nae tawted tyke, tho' e'er sae duddie,
But he wad stan't, as glad to see him,
An' stroan't on stanes an' hillocks wi' him.

The tither was a ploughman's collie –
A rhyming, ranting, raving billie,
Wha for his friend an' comrade had him,
And in his freaks had Luath ca'd him,
After some dog in Highland Sang,*
Was made lang syne, Lord knows how lang.

He was a gash an' faithfu' tyke,
As ever lap a sheugh or dyke.
His honest, sonsie, baws'nt face
Aye gat him friends in ilka place;

* 'Luath, Cuchullin's dog in Ossian's Fingal.' – RB. Luath had been the name of Burns's own dog, a border collie, killed 'by the wanton cruelty of some person', as his brother Gilbert put it, the night before their father died. The poem, begun in 1784, was intended as a tribute to his dog; the other dog, Caesar, a Newfoundland – a newfangled breed – was probably entirely fictional.

His breast was white, his touzie back
Weel clad wi' coat o' glossy black;
His gawsie tail, wi' upward curl,
Hung owre his hurdies wi' a swirl.

Nae doubt but they were fain o' ither,
And unco pack an' thick thegither;
Wi' social nose whiles snuff'd an' snowkit;
Whiles mice an' moudieworts they howkit;
Whiles scour'd awa' in lang excursion,
An' worry'd ither in diversion;
Till tir'd at last wi' mony a farce,
They set them down upon their arse,
An' there began a lang digression
About the 'lords o' the creation'.
Whyles mice and modewurks they howket;
Whyles scour'd awa in lang excursion,
An' worry'd ither in diversion;
Till tir'd at last wi' mony a farce,
They set them down upon their arse,
An' there began a lang digression
About the lords o' the creation.

Caesar

I've aften wonder'd, honest Luath,
What sort o' life poor dogs like you have;
An' when the gentry's life I saw,
What way poor bodies liv'd ava.

Our laird gets in his racked rents,
His coals, his kane, an' a' his stents:
He rises when he likes himsel';
His flunkies answer at the bell;
He ca's his coach; he ca's his horse;
He draws a bonie silken purse,
As lang's my tail, where, thro' the steeks,
The yellow letter'd Geordie keeks.

Frae morn to e'en, it's nought but toiling
At baking, roasting, frying, boiling;
An' tho' the gentry first are stechin,
Yet ev'n the ha' folk fill their pechan
Wi' sauce, ragouts, an' sic like trashtrie,
That's little short o' downright wastrie.
Our whipper-in, wee, blastet wonner,
Poor, worthless elf, it eats a dinner,
Better than ony tenant-man
His Honour has in a' the lan':

An' what poor cot-folk pit their painch in,
I own it's past my comprehension.

Luath

Trowth, Caesar, whiles they're fash't eneugh:
A cottar howkin in a sheugh,
Wi' dirty stanes biggin a dyke,
Bairan a quarry, an' sic like;
Himsel', a wife, he thus sustains,
A smytrie o' wee duddie weans,
An' nought but his han'-daurk, to keep
Them right an' tight in thack an' rape.

An' when they meet wi' sair disasters,
Like loss o' health or want o' masters,
Ye maist wad think, a wee touch langer,
An' they maun starve o' cauld an' hunger:
But how it comes, I never kent yet,
They're maistly wonderfu' contented;
An' buirdly chiels, an' clever hizzies,
Are bred in sic a way as this is.

Caesar

But then, to see how ye're negleckit,
How huff'd, an' cuff'd, an' disrespeckit!
Lord man, our gentry care as little
For delvers, ditchers, an' sic cattle;
They gang as saucy by poor folk,
As I wad by a stinkin brock.

I've notic'd, on our laird's court-day, –
An' mony a time my heart's been wae, –
Poor tenant bodies, scant o' cash,
How they maun thole a factor's snash;
He'll stamp an' threaten, curse an' swear,
He'll apprehend them, poind their gear;
While they maun stan', wi' aspect humble,
An' hear it a', an' fear an' tremble!
I see how folk live that hae riches;
But surely poor-folk maun be wretches!

Luath

They're no sae wretched's ane wad think.
Tho' constantly on poortith's brink,
They're sae accustom'd wi' the sight,
The view o't gives them little fright.

Then chance and fortune are sae guided,
They're aye in less or mair provided:
An' tho' fatigued wi' close employment,
A blink o' rest's a sweet enjoyment.

The dearest comfort o' their lives,
Their grushie weans an' faithfu' wives;
The prattling things are just their pride,
That sweetens a' their fire-side.

An' whiles twalpennie worth o' nappy
Can mak the bodies unco happy:
They lay aside their private cares,
To mind the Kirk and State affairs;
They'll talk o' patronage an' priests,
Wi' kindling fury i' their breasts,
Or tell what new taxation's comin,
An' ferlie at the folk in Lon'on.

As bleak-fac'd Hallowmass returns,
They get the jovial, rantin kirns,
When rural life, of ev'ry station,
Unite in common recreation;
Love blinks, Wit slaps, an' social Mirth
Forgets there's Care upo' the earth.

That merry day the year begins,
They bar the door on frosty win's;
The nappy reeks wi' mantling ream,
An' sheds a heart-inspiring steam;
The luntin pipe, an' sneeshin mill,
Are handed round wi' right guid will;
The cantie auld folks crackin crouse,
The young anes rantin thro' the house –
My heart has been sae fain to see them,
That I for joy hae barkit wi' them.

Still it's owre true that ye hae said,
Sic game is now owre aften play'd;
There's mony a creditable stock
O' decent, honest, fawsont folk,
Are riven out baith root an' branch,
Some rascal's pridefu' greed to quench,
Wha thinks to knit himsel the faster
In favour wi' some gentle master,
Wha, aiblins, thrang a parliamentin,
For Britain's guid his saul indentin –

Caesar

Haith, lad, ye little ken about it:
For Britain's guid! guid faith! I doubt it.
Say rather, gaun as Premiers lead him:
An' saying ay or no's they bid him:
At operas an' plays parading,
Mortgaging, gambling, masquerading:
Or maybe, in a frolic daft,
To Hague or Calais takes a waft,
To mak a tour an' tak a whirl,
To learn *bon ton*, an' see the worl'.

There, at Vienna, or Versailles,
He rives his father's auld entails;
Or by Madrid he takes the rout,
To thrum guitars an' fecht wi' nowt;
Or down Italian vista startles,
Whore-hunting amang groves o' myrtles:
Then bowses drumlie German-water,
To mak himsel look fair an' fatter,
An' clear the consequential sorrows,
Love-gifts of Carnival signoras.
For Britain's guid! for her destruction!
Wi' dissipation, feud, an' faction.

Luath

Hech, man! dear sirs! is that the gate,
They waste sae mony a braw estate!
Are we sae foughten an' harass'd
For gear to gang that gate at last?

O would they stay aback frae courts,
An' please themsels wi' country sports,
It wad for ev'ry ane be better,
The laird, the tenant, an' the cotter!
For thae frank, rantin, ramblin billies,
Fient haet o' them's ill-hearted fellows;
Except for breakin o' their timmer,
Or speakin lightly o' their limmer,
Or shootin of a hare or moor-cock,
The ne'er-a-bit they're ill to poor folk,

But will ye tell me, Master Caesar,
Sure great folk's life's a life o' pleasure?
Nae cauld nor hunger e'er can steer them,
The very thought o't need na fear them.

Caesar

Lord, man, were ye but whiles whare I am,
The gentles, ye wad ne'er envy them!

It's true, they need na starve or sweat,
Thro' winter's cauld, or simmer's heat;
They've nae sair wark to craze their banes,
An' fill auld age wi' grips an' granes:
But human bodies are sic fools,
For a' their colleges an' schools,
That when nae real ills perplex them,
They mak enow themsels to vex them;
An' aye the less they hae to sturt them,
In like proportion, less will hurt them.

A country fellow at the pleugh,
His acre's till'd, he's right eneugh;
A country girl at her wheel,
Her dizzen's dune, she's unco weel;
But gentlemen, an' ladies warst,
Wi' ev'n-down want o' wark are curst.
They loiter, lounging, lank an' lazy;
Tho' deil-haet ails them, yet uneasy;
Their days insipid, dull, an' tasteless;
Their nights unquiet, lang, an' restless.

An' ev'n their sports, their balls an' races,
Their galloping through public places,
There's sic parade, sic pomp an' art,
The joy can scarcely reach the heart.

The men cast out in party-matches,
Then sowther a' in deep debauches.
Ae night they're mad wi' drink an' whoring,
Niest day their life is past enduring.

The ladies arm-in-arm in clusters,
As great an' gracious a' as sisters;
But hear their absent thoughts o' ither,
They're a' run-deils an' jads thegither.
Whiles, owre the wee bit cup an' platie,
They sip the scandal-potion pretty;
Or lee-lang nights, wi' crabbit leuks
Pore owre the devil's pictur'd beuks;
Stake on a chance a farmer's stackyard,
An' cheat like ony unhanged blackguard.

There's some exceptions, man an' woman;
But this is gentry's life in common.

By this, the sun was out of sight,
An' darker gloamin brought the night;
The bum-clock humm'd wi' lazy drone;
The kye stood rowtin i' the loan;
When up they gat an' shook their lugs,
Rejoic'd they werena men but dogs;
An' each took aff his several way,
Resolv'd to meet some ither day.

To A Louse, On Seeing One on a Lady's Bonnet, at Church (1786)

Ha! whaur ye gaun, ye crowlin ferlie?
Your impudence protects you sairly;
I canna say but ye strunt rarely,
   Owre gauze and lace;
Tho', faith! I fear ye dine but sparely
   On sic a place.

Ye ugly, creepin, blastit wonner,
Detested, shunn'd by saunt an' sinner,
How daur ye set your fit upon her –
   Sae fine a lady!

Gae somewhere else and seek your dinner
   On some poor body.

Swith! in some beggar's haffet squattle;
There ye may creep, and sprawl, and sprattle,
Wi' ither kindred, jumping cattle,
   In shoals and nations;
Whaur horn nor bane ne'er daur unsettle
   Your thick plantations.

Now haud you there, ye're out o' sight,
Below the fatt'rels, snug and tight;
Na, faith ye yet! ye'll no be right,
   Till ye've got on it –
The verra tapmost, tow'rin height
   O' Miss's bonnet.

My sooth! right bauld ye set your nose out,
As plump an' grey as ony groset:
O for some rank, mercurial rozet,
   Or fell, red smeddum,
I'd gie you sic a hearty dose o't,
   Wad dress your droddum!

I wad na been surpris'd to spy
You on an auld wife's flainen toy;
Or aiblins some bit duddie boy,
    On's wyliecoat;
But Miss's fine Lunardi, fye!
    How daur ye do't?

O Jeany, dinna toss your head,
An' set your beauties a' abread!
Ye little ken what cursed speed
    The blastie's makin:
Thae winks an' finger-ends, I dread,
    Are notice takin.

O wad some Pow'r the giftie gie us
To see oursels as ithers see us!
It wad frae mony a blunder free us,
    An' foolish notion:
What airs in dress an' gait wad lea'e us,
    An' ev'n devotion!

Epistle To A Young Friend
May —, 1786

I lang hae thought, my youthfu' friend,
A something to have sent you,
Tho' it should serve nae ither end
Than just a kind memento:
But how the subject-theme may gang,
Let time and chance determine;
Perhaps it may turn out a sang:
Perhaps turn out a sermon.

Ye'll try the world soon, my lad;
And, Andrew dear, believe me,
Ye'll find mankind an unco squad,
And muckle they may grieve ye:
For care and trouble set your thought,
Ev'n when your end's attained;
And a' your views may come to nought,
Where ev'ry nerve is strained.

I'll no say, men are villains a';
The real, harden'd wicked,
Wha hae nae check but human law,
Are to a few restricked;
But, Och! mankind are unco weak,
An' little to be trusted;
If self the wavering balance shake,
It's rarely right adjusted!

Yet they wha fa' in Fortune's strife,
Their fate we shouldna censure;
For still, th' important end of life
They equally may answer;
A man may hae an honest heart,
Tho' poortith hourly stare him;
A man may tak a neibor's part,
Yet hae nae cash to spare him.

Aye free, aff-han', your story tell,
When wi' a bosom crony;
But still keep something to yoursel',
Ye scarcely tell to ony:
Conceal yoursel' as weel's ye can
Frae critical dissection;
But keek thro' ev'ry other man,
Wi' sharpen'd, sly inspection.

The sacred lowe o' weel-plac'd love,
Luxuriantly indulge it;
But never tempt th' illicit rove,
Tho' naething should divulge it:
I waive the quantum o' the sin,
The hazard of concealing;
But, Och! it hardens a' within,
And petrifies the feeling!

To catch Dame Fortune's golden smile,
Assiduous wait upon her;
And gather gear by ev'ry wile
That's justified by honour;
Not for to hide it in a hedge,
Nor for a train attendant;
But for the glorious privilege
Of being independent.

The fear o' Hell's a hangman's whip,
To haud the wretch in order;
But where ye feel your honour grip,
Let that aye be your border;
Its slightest touches, instant pause –
Debar a' side-pretences,
And resolutely keep its laws,
Uncaring consequences.

The great Creator to revere,
Must sure become the creature;
But still the preaching cant forbear,
And ev'n the rigid feature:
Yet ne'er with wits profane to range,
Be complaisance extended;

An atheist-laugh's a poor exchange
For Deity offended!

When ranting round in pleasure's ring,
Religion may be blinded;
Or if she gie a random sting,
It may be little minded;
But when on life we're tempest-driv'n –
A conscience but a canker –
A correspondence fix'd wi' Heav'n,
Is sure a noble anchor!

Adieu, dear, amiable youth!
Your heart can ne'er be wanting!
May Prudence, Fortitude and Truth
Erect your brow undaunting!
In ploughman phrase 'God send you speed,'
Still daily to grow wiser;
And may ye better reck the rede
Than ever did th'Adviser!

Strathallan's Lament

(1787)

Thickest night, o'erhang my dwelling!
Howling tempests, o'er me rave!
Turbid torrents, wintry swelling,
Roaring by my lonely cave!

Crystal streamlets gently flowing,
Busy haunts of base mankind,
Western breezes softly blowing,
Suit not my distracted mind.

In the cause of Right engaged,
Wrongs injurious to redress,
Honour's war we strongly waged,
But the Heavens denied success.

Ruin's wheel has driven o'er us,
Not a hope that dare attend,
The wide world is all before us –
But a world without a friend.

Address To The Toothache

(1786)

My curse upon your venom'd stang,
That shoots my tortur'd gums alang,
An' thro' my lug gies mony a twang,
   Wi' gnawing vengeance,
Tearing my nerves wi' bitter pang,
   Like racking engines!

When fevers burn, or ague freezes,
Rheumatics gnaw, or colic squeezes,
Our neibor's sympathy can ease us,
   Wi' pitying moan;
But thee – thou hell o' a' diseases –
   Aye mocks our groan.

Adown my beard the slavers trickle
I throw the wee stools o'er the mickle,
While round the fire the giglets keckle,
   To see me loup,
While, raving mad, I wish a heckle
   Were in their doup!

In a' the numerous human dools,
Ill hairsts, daft bargains, cutty stools,
Or worthy frien's rak'd i' the mools, –
   Sad sight to see!
The tricks o' knaves, or fash o' fools,
   Thou bear'st the gree!

Where'er that place be priests ca' hell,
Where a' the tones o' misery yell,
An' ranked plagues their numbers tell,
   In dreadfu' raw,
Thou, Toothache, surely bear'st the bell,
   Amang them a'!

O thou grim, mischief-making chiel,
That gars the notes o' discord squeel,
Till daft mankind aft dance a reel
   In gore, a shoe-thick,
Gie a' the faes o' Scotland's weal
   A towmond's toothache!

A Red, Red Rose
(1794)

O my Luve's like a red, red rose,
That's newly sprung in June:
O my Luve's like the melodie,
That's sweetly play'd in tune.

As fair art thou, my bonie lass,
So deep in luve am I;
And I will luve thee still, my dear,
Till a' the seas gang dry.

Till a' the seas gang dry, my dear,
And the rocks melt wi' the sun;
And I will luve thee still, my dear,
While the sands o' life shall run.

And fare-thee-weel, my only Luve!
And fare-thee-weel, a while!
And I will come again, my Luve,
Tho' 'twere ten thousand mile!

The Banks O' Doon

(1792)

(Third version)

Ye banks and braes o' bonie Doon,
How can ye bloom sae fresh and fair?
How can ye chant, ye little birds,
And I sae weary fu' o' care!
Thou'll break my heart, thou warbling bird,
That wantons thro' the flowering thorn:
Thou minds me o' departed joys,
Departed never to return.

Aft hae I rov'd by bonie Doon,
To see the rose and woodbine twine:
And ilka bird sang o' its luve,
And fondly sae did I o' mine;
Wi' lightsome heart I pu'd a rose,
Fu' sweet upon its thorny tree!
And my fause luver staw my rose,
But ah! he left the thorn wi' me.

Ae Fond Kiss, And Then We Sever

(1791)

Ae fond kiss, and then we sever;
Ae fareweel, alas, for ever!
Deep in heart-wrung tears I'll pledge thee,
Warring sighs and groans I'll wage thee.

Who shall say that Fortune grieves him,
While the star of hope she leaves him?
Me, nae cheerful twinkle lights me;
Dark despair around benights me.

I'll ne'er blame my partial fancy,
Naething could resist my Nancy:
But to see her was to love her;
Love but her, and love for ever.

Had we never lov'd sae kindly,
Had we never lov'd sae blindly,
Never met – or never parted,
We had ne'er been broken-hearted.

Fare-thee-weel, thou first and fairest!
Fare-thee-weel, thou best and dearest!
Thine be ilka joy and treasure,
Peace, Enjoyment, Love and Pleasure!

Ae fond kiss, and then we sever!
Ae fareweel, alas, for ever!
Deep in heart-wrung tears I'll pledge thee,
Warring sighs and groans I'll wage thee.

Afton Water ('Sweet Afton')
(1792)

Flow gently, sweet Afton, amang thy green braes;
Flow gently, I'll sing thee a song in thy praise;
My Mary's asleep by thy murmuring stream,
Flow gently, sweet Afton, disturb not her dream.
Thou stock-dove whose echo resounds through the glen,
Ye wild whistling blackbirds in yon thorny den,
Thou green-crested lapwing, thy screaming forbear;
I charge you disturb not my slumbering fair.

How lofty, sweet Afton, thy neighbouring hills,
Far mark'd with the courses of clear-winding rills;
There daily I wander as noon rises high,
My flocks and my Mary's sweet cot in my eye.

How pleasant thy banks and green valleys below,
Where wild in the woodlands the primroses blow;
There oft as mild ev'ning weeps over the lea,
The sweet-scented birk shades my Mary and me.

Thy crystal stream, Afton, how lovely it glides,
And winds by the cot where my Mary resides;
How wanton thy waters her snowy feet lave,
As, gathering sweet flowerets, she stems thy clear wave.

Flow gently, sweet Afton, amang thy green braes;
Flow gently, sweet river, the theme of my lays;
My Mary's asleep by thy murmuring stream,
Flow gently, sweet Afton, disturb not her dream.

Lines on Fergusson, the Poet
(1792)

Ill-fated genius! Heaven-taught Fergusson!
What heart that feels and will not yield a tear,
To think Life's sun did set e'er well begun
To shed its influence on thy bright career.

O why should truest Worth and Genius pine
Beneath the iron grasp of Want and Woe,
While titled knaves and idiot-Greatness shine
In all the splendour Fortune can bestow?

Robert Bruce's March To Bannockburn
('Scots, Wha Hae')
(1793)

Scots, wha hae wi' Wallace bled,
Scots, wham Bruce has aften led,
Welcome to your gory bed,
   Or to Victorie!

Now's the day, and now's the hour:
See the front o' battle lour;
See approach proud Edward's power –
   Chains and Slaverie!

Wha will be a traitor knave?
Wha can fill a coward's grave?
Wha sae base as be a slave?
   Let him turn and flee!

Wha, for Scotland's King and Law,
Freedom's sword will strongly draw,
Freeman stand, or Freeman fa',
   Let him on wi' me!

By Oppression's woes and pains!
By your sons in servile chains!
We will drain our dearest veins,
   But they shall be free!

Lay the proud usurpers low!
Tyrants fall in every foe!
Liberty's in every blow! –
   Let us do or die!

A Man's A Man For A' That
(1795)

Is there for honest poverty
That hings his head, an' a' that;
The coward slave – we pass him by,
We dare be poor for a' that!
For a' that, an' a' that,
Our toils obscure an' a' that,
The rank is but the guinea's stamp,
The man's the gowd for a' that.

What tho' on hamely fare we dine,
Wear hoddin grey, an' a that;
Gie fools their silks, and knaves
    their wine;
A man's a man for a' that:
For a' that, an' a' that,
Their tinsel show, an' a' that;
The honest man, tho' e'er sae poor,
Is king o' men for a' that.

Ye see yon birkie ca'd a lord,
Wha struts, an' stares, an' a' that;

Tho' hundreds worship at his word,
He's but a coof for a' that:
For a' that, an' a' that,
His ribband, star, an' a' that:
The man o' independent mind
He looks an' laughs at a' that.

A prince can mak a belted knight,
A marquis, duke, an' a' that;
But an honest man's aboon his might,
Gude faith, he mauna fa' that!
For a' that, an' a' that,
Their dignities an' a' that;
The pith o' sense, an' pride o' worth,
Are higher rank than a' that.

Then let us pray that come it may –
As come it will for a' that –
That sense and worth, o'er a' the earth,
Shall bear the gree, an' a' that.
For a' that, an' a' that,
It's coming yet for a' that,
That man to man, the world o'er,
Shall brothers be for a' that.

Auld Lang Syne

(1788)

Should auld acquaintance be forgot,
   And never brought to mind?
Should auld acquaintance be forgot,
   And auld lang syne!

> CHORUS – *For auld lang syne, my dear,*
>   *For auld lang syne.*
> *We'll tak a cup o' kindness yet,*
>   *For auld lang syne.*

And surely ye'll be your pint stowp!
   And surely I'll be mine!
And we'll tak a cup o'kindness yet,
   For auld lang syne.
     For auld, &c.

We twa hae run about the braes,
   And pou'd the gowans fine;
But we've wander'd mony a weary fit,
   Sin' auld lang syne.
     For auld, &c.

We twa hae paidl'd in the burn,
  Frae morning sun till dine;
But seas between us braid hae roar'd
  Sin' auld lang syne.
    For auld, &c.

And there's a hand, my trusty fiere!
  And gie's a hand o' thine!
And we'll tak a right gude-willie waught,
  For auld lang syne.
    For auld, &c.

Kirkudbright Grace

Some have meat and cannot eat,
  Some cannot eat that want it:
But we have meat and we can eat,
  Sae let the Lord be thankit.

GLOSSARY OF WORDS

aboon, **abon** – above, up

ae – one

aff-hand, at once

agley – awry

aiblins – perhaps

airns – irons

aits – oats

ava – at all

awnie – bearded

bawk – a field path

baws'nt – white-streaked

bear – barley

bide – abide, endure

billies – fellow, comrade, brother

birk – birch

bleezing – blazing

blellum – a babbler; a blusterer

boddle – a farthing

bonie – bonnie, pretty, beautiful

braw – handsome, fine, gaily dressed

brawlie – finely, perfectly, heartily

buirdly – stout, stalwart

brunstane – brimstone

byke – a bee hive; a swarm; a crowd

cantie – cheerful, merry

cantraip – magic, witching

carlin, **carline** – an old woman; a beldam, a witch

chapman – a pedlar

chiel, **chield** (i. e. child) – a fellow, a young fellow

cit – a citizen; a merchant

claes – clothes

clankie – a severe knock

claught – clutched, seized

cleekit – linked arms

coft – bought

Coil, Coila – RB's part of Ayrshire

coof – a dolt, a ninny; a dastard

coost (i. e. cast) – threw off, tossed

core – corps

cour – fold, lower

couthie – couthy, loving, affable, cosy, comfortable

crack – talk

cranreuch – hoar-frost

creeshie – greasy

crouse – cheerful, courageous

crowlin – crawling

crummock, **cummock** – a cudgel, a crooked staff

cushat – the woodpigeon

cutty – short

cutty-stools – stools of repentance

daffin – larking, fun

daurk – task, a day's labour

deave – to deafen

dight – wipe, clean

dirl – ring, rattle

doited – muddled, doting; stupid, bewildered

dool – sorrow

douce, douse – sedate, sober, prudent

doup – the bottom

doylt – stupid, stupefied

droddum – the breech, rump

drouthy – thirsty

drumlie – muddy, turbid

dub – puddle, slush

duddie – ragged; duds, duddies – rags

eldritch – unearthly, haunted, fearsome

ettle – aim

ev'n-down – downright

fand – found

fatt'rels – ribbon ends

fause – false

fawsont – seemly, well-doing; good-looking

fecht – fight

ferlie – 'wonder, a term of contempt' (RB)

feint haet – 'of negation, nothing' (RB)

fient – fiend

fiere – brother, friend

flainen, flannen – flannel

flang – flung

foggage – rank grass

fou, fow – full (i. e. of drink)

fyke – to fret, fuss; fidget

gang – to go

gart – made

gash – wise

gate – road, way, manner

gawsie – buxom; jolly.

gear – money, wealth; goods; stuff

Geordie – guinea (dim. of George, George III's head being on the coin)

ghaist – ghost

giglets – giggling youngsters or maids

gled – a hawk, a kite

glunch – frown, growl

gowd – gold

gowans – daisies

graith – implements, gear; furniture; attire

gree – the prize (degree)

groset, grozet – a gooseberry

grushie – thriving

gude/guid-willie – hearty, full of good-will

haet – a thing

haffet – side of the head

hairst – harvest

hald – home, possession

han'-daurk – *see* daurk

hizzies – a hussy, a wench

hoddin – rough woollen fabric

hotch'd – jerked

houlet, howlet – owl

howk – dig

hurdies – 'the loins, the crupper' (RB)

icker – an ear of corn

ilk, ilka – each, every

jad – a jade

jaup – splash about

kail – kale; cabbage; Scots' broth

kane – rents in kind

keckle – to cackle, to giggle

keek – look, glance

kirn – a churn

knowe – knoll

kyte – belly

laith – loath

laverock – lav'rock, the lark

leeze me on – an endearment;
   blessings on; commend me to

loup – leap

lowe – flame

luggie – dish, bowl

lug –ear

luntin – smoking

mailen – mailin, a farm

maskin-pat – teapot

maun – must

mear – a mare

meikle, mickle, muckle – much, great

melder – a grinding corn

mirk – dark

mools – graves

moudieworts – moles

muckle – *see* meikle

nappy – ale, liquor

nieve – fist

nit – nut

olio – spicy Mediterranean stew

painch – paunch

parritch – porridge

pattle – a ploughstaff

pechan – the stomach

pin – skewer

placads – proclamations

plack – four pennies (Scots)

poind – to seize, to impound

poortith – poverty

pussie – a hare (also a cat)

quean – a young woman, a lass

rape – a rope

rant – to rollick, to roister

ream – to cream, to foam

reek – smoke

rigwoodie – lean

rive – to burst, split, break

rozet – resin

sark – a shirt

saucy – fastidiously

saul – soul

sconner – disgust

scrievin – careering

shachl'd – shapeless

sheugh – a ditch, a furrow; gutter

skellum – a good-for-nothing

skelp – slap, smack

skinking – watery

smeddum – a powder

smiddie – smithy

smoor'd – smothered

smytrie – a small collection; a litter

snash – abuse

sned – to lop, to prune

sneeshin-mill – snuff-box

snell – bitter, biting

snowkit – snuffed

sonsie, sonsy – pleasant, good-natured, jolly

sowther – to solder

spean – to wean

sprattle – scramble

squattle – to squat; to settle

staw – to surfeit; to sicken; stole

stechin – cramming

steeks – stitches

stents – assessments, dues

stibble – stubble

stoure – dust; storm, commotion

stowp – jug

stroan't – 'to spout, to piss' (RB)

strunt – swagger

sturt – worry, trouble

swall'd – swelled

swats – new ale

tapsalteerie – topsy-turvy

tassie – a goblet

tawted – matted

thack and rape – (thatch and rope) home necessities

thairm – small tripes

thir – these

thole – to endure; to suffer

thrang – busy; thronging in crowds; a throng

thrave – twenty-four sheaves of corn

thraw – to twist; to turn; to thwart

thrissle – thistle

timmer – timber; material

tinkler – tinker

tint – lost

tippenny – twopenny ale

touzie, towzie – shaggy

towmond – a twelvemonth

trashtrie – small trash

troke – to barter

unco – remarkable, uncommon; remarkably, uncommonly, excessively

usquabae – whisky

vauntie – proud

wale – choice, to choose

walie, wawlie – choice; ample, large

wame – the belly

war'ly – worldly

wastrie – waste

waught – draught, swig

waulie – jolly

weanies – babies

wha – who

whalpit – whelped

whins – gorse bushes

whissle – whistle

winnock – window

wonner – a wonder

wyliecoat – undervest

INDEX OF FIRST LINES